Reinhard Illner

To The Class of 2030

A Letter and Apology

Title cover photo: Lily, from the class of 2030

Title cover design: Teresita Hernandez-Quesada

"We do not inherit the earth from our ancestors;
we borrow it from our children."

Chief Seattle

Contents

Chapter 1

Prologue

As I started writing this in the spring of 2012, you were about to be born, or an infant, and blissfully unaware of the problems your society and planet faces. Your presence in 2030 is our future, and to a large extent it is ours to shape. Few people now care or worry about this fact, although we read things like "...the accumulated debt of the United States (about 16 trillion dollars, at this point, and growing rapidly) is a liability for future generations." True enough, it is. But it isn't our problem. Or is there some moral reason why we should be concerned? And should we take action of some kind to address the issue? And what can we do anyway?

The example of accumulating debt is only one of a number of big issues which will impact your life. I am writing this letter because I do worry and care, and my main purpose is a gathering of a list of such issues, discuss them in detail, and explore avenues of resolution which are or, mostly, are not being taken. There is a fair amount of variation in these problems as you compare different countries or societies; much of what will be discussed applies transparently to the United States, and, to a lesser degree, to Canada and the United Kingdom. However, troubling symptoms of political, sociological and environmental collapse are visible all over the world.

It is my firm conviction that in many serious cases the steps taken by those in power are either inadequate or lead completely in the wrong direction, with dire consequences for you. There are many like myself who see the problems presented in this book as urgent and serious, and who push for action. Sadly, their voices are barely listened to, and their efforts are largely obstructed by inertia or even active resistance. Current political developments in many countries, in particular the United States, Canada and some European countries, often logically entail poor fiscal and environmental choices, and lead simultaneously to erosion of democratic structures and values. Side effects are appalling inequity in distribution of wealth, environmental degradation, and growing levels of illiteracy. At the core of these developments are beliefs that are contrary to what I would call "community spirit" and "generational contracts"; it will become clear as you read on that these beliefs foster an atmosphere in which governments are either deprived of the power to meet their mandate, namely, serving the community by providing infrastructure, education, health services and so on, or, worse, are made accomplices to powers which are effectively controlling the economy of whole countries. The banking sector of the U.S. is a prominent example, and not the only one.

This development is a nightmarish return to 19th century standards in society organization and structure, and it is being accepted without much resistance. Unless the society of this second decade of the 21st century realizes the slippery slope on which it finds itself and takes action to move off it, you, the class of 2030, are likely to find yourself in a world in which resources are scarce, the environment is severely damaged, democratic structures are compromised, quality education and health care are only available to the rich, and good jobs are few and far between. The implications for your future are bleak. In contrast, 60 years ago, less than a decade after the greatest war the world had ever seen, most countries that are now known as "first world" were poorer than now, but there were a lot of professional options, and social systems assuring free or inexpensive high level education and affordable health care for all were universal. Environmental problems existed but were far less recognized than today, and they did not pose such large-scale threats to the planetary equilibrium and its human guests as they do today.

Let us go through a quick review of what happened in these 60 years, and how it led to the state of the world you have grown up in. In the 1950s and 1960s favourable economic conditions and the social contracts between manufacturers, governments and employees generated an unprecedented economic expansion. First signs of trouble emerged in the 1970s with two subsequent oil crises. The rapid growth of energy consumption in the west had led to a dependency on oil imports from the Middle East and other countries (Venezuela, Nigeria, Indonesia, and a few others) which left western countries subject to political and economic pressures by the suppliers. The logical consequence would have been to try and mitigate these dependencies, and efforts to this end were first made in the United States under the Carter administration. Sadly, these efforts were abandoned when Reagan became president; there can be no doubt that the U.S. oil industry used their new-found clout to protect their financial interests by ensuring that the U.S. would remain as dependent on fossil fuels, especially oil, as it had become during the previous decades.

In the 1980s the neoconservative revolution went further-it was openly asserted (by Ronald Reagan and his admirers) that too much government was bad, that the markets would sort out problems by themselves, and that the most important step towards a blissful state of prosperity and freedom would be tax cuts, less government, and reduced social services. In fact, the Reagan administration cut taxes mostly for the rich, and compensated with tax increases for the middle class[1]. Growing deficits during this period were largely due to dramatic increases in defence spending; the accumulated debt of the U.S. tripled during the Reagan administration, to a total of 2 trillion dollars.

These developments were paralleled or followed by a deregulation of the financial industry. Laws in place since the 1930s (and, like the Glass–Steagall act, created to prevent a repeat of the crash of 1929) were gradually revoked

---

[1] see TEFRA: Tax Equity and Fiscal Responsibility Act of 1982

and allowed the emergence of waves of speculation not seen since the 1920s. Within a few short years the markets lost stability, and market crashes or economic/ financial crises occurred with disturbing frequency, often piggybacking each other. The most prominent examples, still haunting the world as I write this, were the evil twins: the housing bubble which collapsed in 2007-2008, leading to the financial crisis of 2008. Now, in 2013, as you are an infant, the world has still not recovered from the recession this caused. Your parents and grandparents had to shoulder losses of trillions of dollars, money ultimately coming out of your inheritance. Your parents' generation is directly and indirectly indebted on many levels: For example, federal, provincial (or state) and municipal deficits are piling up and will have to be paid off in some way (the traditional tool to do this is inflation). Then there are the individual debts—mortgages, lines of credit, loans, credit card debts. The total debt load of the United States of America, counting all these levels of debt, is in excess of 50 trillion dollars as I write these lines.

There are other ugly legacies you are left with from our generation. The environment has changed—our casual use of fossil fuels has raised the CO_2 level in the atmosphere to above 430 ppm, 30% more than in the middle of the 20th century. You are living with the consequences- melted permafrost in the Arctic, diminishing glaciers in the high mountain ranges, shrinking ice sheets in Greenland and the Arctic. It appears that there are more violent storms with flooding, stronger hurricanes and tornadoes, and there seem to be more and stronger heat waves and droughts. Global food production is already adversely affected. The upper water levels in the oceans suffer from acidification due to the increased carbon dioxide levels, and plankton, coral reefs, shellfish and the attached food chain are all under stress. The oceans are rising.

All of this is already happening now, but there is obstruction and denial by industrial players, notably the fossil fuel industries, whose balance sheets are endangered (or so they think) by climate actions. As a consequence, they have launched huge public relations campaigns and are making massive efforts to influence government policies to keep the status quo. This is short-sighted and potentially disastrous, but it works for the time being. It works against YOUR interests.

You have likely grown up in suburbia, and the world you have known consists of endless rows of homes, some of them individual houses, many others townhouses, apartments or high-rises. The monotony is interrupted by strip malls, in which retail stores (many of them mega-stores) compete for the dollars you have to spend. Much of your city is not accessible to you, because it is hidden behind the walls of gated communities, private industry or government facilities. My generation used to have fairly easy access to what we called "nature"— we had the option to leave the city (by car, bicycle, bus or train) and go hiking in the woods, explore wild rivers, or walk between fields where wheat was grown or cows grazed. These choices are greatly reduced: private interests have developed much of the land to such a degree that your recreational options are reduced to mostly organized activities, many in artificial environments, others in outdoor but controlled environments like golf courses or theme parks.

In short, your freedoms, be it the freedom for intellectual or economical development, or the freedom to just explore your world, have been greatly compromised by the choices of my generation, and, perversely, the quest for freedom was frequently quoted by decision makers when these choices were made.

Granted, the vast majority of this generation did not see it this way. Yet the facts speak for themselves, and the purpose of my writing is to lay them out. Maybe it will be a factor in the formation of critical public awareness needed to address the problems. However, truth be told, I have little hope that my writing can make a difference, but at least it will show that I cared. You may also take it as an apology for my generation, a generation that knew Chief Seattle's words but paid no heed.

Victoria, British Columbia
Summer 2013

Chapter 2

A Subversion of Democracy

2.1 Invasion and Perversion of Democratic Institutions by Special Interests

Special interest groups have always made efforts to gain and use influence in government to their own advantage. Classical examples of such groups are trade unions representing classes of workers or public employees, or conglomerates of, say, companies whose products are of central importance (coal and steel are examples which mattered in the early 20th century; oil and gas more so at the present). In functional democracies of decades (and centuries) past, the power of the elected government was generally such that these efforts were held in check, but history is also replete of examples where special interest groups aligned themselves with extreme parties to overcome democratic procedures, to the detriment of all. What is happening at this present time is a (troubling) development in which spe-

cial interest groups are using their significant numbers, their
financial strengths, or their control over the media to gain
control over governing institutions. I will describe four such
groups which are active in North America and beyond; in
fact, although their origins are vastly different, these groups
have learned to co-ordinate their forces to control the U.S.
Congress, with results that basically paralyze the U.S. government. The prospects for your future are very bleak—if
current developments continue, it may very well be that by
2030 you will live in a democracy only by name, because
your lawmakers will in essence be manipulated, at all time,
by special interests.

The first group on my list has been recognized for a long
time and is often called "the military-industrial complex" [1],
a coalition of industrial and military interests which has become such a powerful and resourceful player in Washington
(and by similar arrangements, with their counterparts in
many other industrial countries) that they wield an undue
influence on government decisions. In 2003 it was largely
this group which coerced the American public (as repre-
sented in Congress) to engage in an unnecessary and very
bloody war (of aggression!) in Iraq. The war took thousands of lives, maimed tens of thousands, and cost hundreds
of billions of dollars; it was a major contributor to the dramatic escalation in government debt after 2003. In retro-
spect, it is very worth while to read or listen to President
Eisenhower's Farewell Address, words spoken on television
on January 17, 1961. From our present point of view his

---

[1]this term was used in President D. D. Eisenhower's Farewell Address

words seem nothing less than prophetic.

We ... must avoid the impulse to live only for today, plundering for our own ease and convenience the precious resources of tomorrow. We cannot mortgage the material assets of our grandchildren without risking the loss also of their political and spiritual heritage. We want democracy to survive for all generations to come, not to become the insolvent phantom of tomorrow.

Read carefully, Class of 2030. He was talking about you! And he went on:

... we must guard against the acquisition of unwarranted influence, whether sought or unsought, by the military-industrial complex. The potential for the disastrous rise of misplaced power exists and will persist. We must never let the weight of this combination endanger our liberties or democratic processes. We should take nothing for granted. Only an alert and knowledgeable citizenry can compel the proper meshing of the huge industrial and military machinery of defence with our peaceful methods and goals, so that security and liberty may prosper together.

So there. He saw it more than 50 years ago, and he warned us. And yet the American people and much of the rest of the free world were deceived in the Iraq war, and still there are those who defend this war. The military-industrial complex is alive and well, and working for its own interests with all the immense power and resources at its disposal.

A second group, with some overlap with the first, is the financial industry, often simply referred to as "Wall Street." It is a fact that the financial institutions which are the building blocks of "Wall Street" have enough power to force the U.S. government to bail them out when financial speculations go wrong. This, in a nutshell, is what happened after the financial crisis of 2008. There are many millions of people in the U.S. (and in many other countries) who lost their houses and savings as a consequence of the financial bubble; most found little or no support by their government; but many of those who had created and traded the toxic assets were saved with public money amounting to more that $ 700 billion- the TARP program. The argument was that the financial system would collapse otherwise. Well, nobody could really check: the U.S. government was effectively run by those who had caused the problems to begin with. They were, naturally, more interested in saving their own skin than those of the millions of investors who lost their houses and livelihoods.

It is thus a sad reality that your parents or grandparents lost a significant fraction of their wealth due to the manipulations of Wall Street, and this happened with the blessings and to some extent with the support of the government. Investment and commercial banks were deregulated to such an extent that they were able to speculate with the most opaque and risky of financial instruments- derivatives of stock and commodity markets, collateral debt obligations, credit default swaps, derivatives of the previous, and so on. The public (your parents and grandparents) were deceived, by smoke and mirrors so to speak, to go into debt they could not afford, buy real estate they did not need, and invest in the above risky assets. When the bubble burst, the American public was suddenly trillions of dollars poorer; but nobody was really ever held accountable. The missing money is a significant factor in the huge public and private debt you were born with.

The details of this catastrophe have been well documented in many books and articles. One of the best is [4].

The third group is less well defined. In essence, it is a loose assortment of wealthy people and businesses who are trying to opt out of community obligations by only serving their own interests. This happens either by direct attempts of manipulating the government, or by efforts to reduce taxes. I will address the tax matter in detail in the next section, but will here briefly write about government manipulation.

The U.S. "enjoys" a system in which lawmakers are easily accessible to special interests. This is known as the lobby system, or, as the conservative commentator Lou Dobbs has put it, "the best government money can buy" [2]. Unbelievable amounts of money are spent by corporate America to convince lawmakers to vote "their" way. Publicly available data on lobbying [6] provide the following approximate amounts of money spent on lobbying efforts (*excluding* campaign contributions) by the top lobbying sectors from 1998 to 2012:

FIRE sector (Finance, Insurance, Real Estate) :	$ 5,215,446,384
Health (Pharmaceutical Industry, Hospitals):	$ 5,242,060,866
Miscellaneous Business:	$ 5,281,233,641
Communications/Electronics:	$ 4,329,167,814
Energy and Natural Resources:	$ 3,890,250,684

This list is just the very top, yet the amounts already add up to more than 23 billion. You can see how the financial muscle of Goldman Sachs, Exxon Mobil, Pfizer Pharmaceuticals, General Motors and countless others is bending the arm of your government. There are wealthy law firms whose existence depends to a large extent on their services to the lobbying needs of business. Their clients subscribe to these services in order to gain tax advantages, protection from competition, exemptions from regulation, or direct subsidies. An example which has recently found much attention in the news is the NRA (National Rifle Association), which, through its influence in Congress, has just successfully blocked legislation which would have made it harder to obtain assault rifles, or create mandatory background checks for gun purchases. The Senate rebuttal of such legislation was called "shameful" by President Obama and many supporters; polls suggest that a massive majority of Americans is supportive of more gun control, yet the NRA had their way. This, in spite of ongoing massacres by deranged young men, who use military style assault weapons to kill children and other innocents at schools or universities.

The fourth and last group to be included here are fundamentalist Christians. The character of this movement is radically different from the previous examples inasmuch as its members are not driven by financial greed, but rather by faith or ultra-conservative values. At first glance this seems a more noble stance; however, it is in a way more dangerous because this movement is not just trying to amass wealth—they desire to change society. To mention a well known and notorious example, they are trying in earnest to change school curricula to challenge the teaching of the theory of evolution in favour of the biblical story of creation. In this effort they are clashing with scientists and government officials whose mandate is to guarantee a school education free of religious or ideological prejudice.

A dangerous and troubling side effect of the growing political clout of fundamentalist Christians is the implicit animosity towards adherents of other religions, or more generally all those who question or resist the fundamentalist agenda. And as I write this, there are conservative politicians who openly support this agenda in order to attract the many votes the fundamentalists have to offer. Rick Santorum, who was one of the leading contenders for the Republican presidential nomination, and who many see as a future contender, was in the spring of 2012 openly campaigning to those who ..." believe in the bible and own a gun". He, and most others in his camp, wish to make abortion illegal and oppose gay marriage. And they find massive support in the American south and midwest. [7]

The latter two groups have given birth to a strange and confused, yet very powerful political entity: the Tea Party. It is hard to see how the various interests which push this movement can find agreement; chances are they are a "marriage of convenience", united more by what they oppose rather than what they wish to achieve. As the name suggests, they wish to turn back the wheel of history and return America to a time when government was far away, when education lay mostly in the hands of the church, and when the bible and a gun where integral parts of every household. Indeed, there are politicians running for office who declare this as a desirable state of affairs. If they gain power, you may find that your options for a liberal education and free, unencumbered political discourse were flushed out before you started school.

In 2012, as the Republican Party searched for a candidate to challenge President Barack Obama, several conservative U.S. politicians spoke out on behalf of or ran directly as representatives for the Tea Party. First and foremost among those was Sarah Palin, who emerged as the darling of new right and was frequently featured on the conservative Fox News. In the end she decided not to enter the Republican field of presidential candidates; among those who did were Michele Bachmann, the previously mentioned Rick Santorum and Rick Perry, the present governor of Texas. What united these people was their belief in the universal power of tax cuts, their disdain for social programs and social justice, and their invocations of religious beliefs in the sense of fundamentalist Christianity. These beliefs enter their political agenda on many fronts, for example in their opposition of legalized abortion, opposition to gay and lesbian marriage, or their labelling of different religious or ethnic minorities. They were also anti-science because their religious foundations clash with modern scientific evidence. While none from this group succeeded in gaining the Republican nomination, they forced others, in particular the eventual candidate Mitt Romney, to move their agenda to the right in order to seize some of the ultraconservative votes.

Other contenders for the Republican nomination distinguished themselves by ignorance and hypocrisy. Nobody may remember now, but Herman Cain's grip on geography was so shaky that he thought Libya was governed by the Taliban. And his socioeconomic agenda? Here is what he said, famously, while running for the Republican presidential nomination in the fall of 2011:

Don't blame Wall Street, don't blame the big banks. If you don't have a job and you are not rich, blame yourself!

Well, you may think of this whatever you wish, but Herman Cain was at least honest. Many other Republicans refrained from saying such things, but their actions (or, in many cases, lack of) showed that they shared his beliefs. They lost the election, but their agenda persists.

The show which the Republican nomination spectacle provided in the spring of 2012 was entertaining and depressing at the same time. Regrettably, political trends in other countries pointed into the same troubling direction. In Canada, the governing Conservative Party, under the leadership of Stephen Harper, displayed behaviour which can hardly be considered acceptable under democratic rules. As I write this, scientists and public servants whose opinions or work is in conflict with Harper's agenda are muzzled or dismissed; the government works with negative ads and branding of critics to push its agenda, an agenda in uncritical support of the Alberta oil producers. This is, of course, linked to the environmental crisis which is already visiting our world as I write, and which is the topic of Chapter 4.

2.2   Taxation, and why it isn't happening

2.2.1   The 1980s: A conservative landslide

The 1970s and 1980s saw vigorous competition between conservative and social democratic forces in many countries of the western world. This competition was healthy inasmuch as both sides had good arguments for their case, and they had the Soviet Union and its satellites as a model for real existing socialism (communism) with all its (many) problems, and its strengths. The problems were severe—there were constraints of many basic freedoms (speech, travel, political organization), there were endemic economic problems (shortages, poor distribution) and a rigid ideology (the idea of world revolution, oppression of other ideas, the cold war). The system was also not really social: there were privileged classes in all the countries of the Soviet Bloc. However, there also were universal health and child care, and a good education system.

The west was in competition with and afraid of this system. Social democratic parties and movements in western Europe, North America and the Far East defined their programs as committed to democracy and freedom while providing universal social services. This worked as long as economies were thriving, and it is still working in many countries (for example, in Scandinavia). With repeated economic contractions (starting with the oil crises) the social systems became expensive, and many countries started to make adjustments in order to balance their budgets.

Conservative forces (led by Margaret Thatcher in Britain, Ronald Reagan in the US, the Christian Democrats in Germany) focussed their programs on the lack of freedom in state-planned economies in the Soviet bloc, and pushed their agenda with slogans like "Freedom or Socialism"[2] or "Government is not the solution to our problem. Government *is* the problem"[3]. These catchy phrases suggested to the voters that a) You could not have freedom if you chose socialism, or, if you valued your freedom, you had to reject socialism (for the validity of such assertions, I recommend that you ask people from Scandinavia, or France, or Holland...), and b) Government was inefficient, wasteful, inept and corrupt, and needed to be held in check. In particular, government deserved very little of your money and trust.

The voters bought it. In the 1980s, conservative governments were in place in the US (Reagan), the UK (Thatcher), Germany (Kohl), Canada (Mulroney) and many other western democracies.

This political change brought promises and actions of tax reduction. The philosophy was that governments tended to

---

[2]CDU/ CSU slogan, 1976
[3]Ronald Reagan inaugural address, January 20, 1981

use tax dollars poorly and wastefully, and that the money would create more jobs and more wealth if left in private hands. And there was some truth in that. However, what happened was that the powerful, newly elected conservative governments tended to "throw the baby out with the bath water:" The suddenly reduced taxes (at all levels: income tax, corporate tax, capital gains taxes, etc.) left more money in private pockets but led to severe shortages in government programs, except, in America, in defence spending. As a consequence, social and health care programs were cut, with the inevitable hardships for the poor and the lower middle class. These cuts were insufficient to balance budgets, and the Reagan administration began to run deficits which were described "a flat and dangerous failure" by the media.

The 1981 tax cuts of the Reagan administration were rationalized with arguments from the supply-side economics movement, a movement formed in opposition to Keynesian demand-stimulus economics. It was argued that reduced taxes would lead to economic stimulus and ultimately *increased* government revenue. The Economic Recovery Tax Act of 1981 included an across-the-board decrease in the marginal income tax rates in the U.S. by 23% over three years, with the top rate falling from 70% to 50% and the bottom rate dropping from 14% to 11%. Estate and corporate taxes dropped by $150 billion over a five year period. TEFRA, The Tax Equity and Fiscal Responsibility Act of 1982, rescinded some of the cuts from 1981 in order to deal with the revenue shortfall caused by the continuing weak economy [8], but the bulk of the damage had been done, and the tax system had effectively been modified in such a way as to favour the rich.

Yet, most Americans lived in the conviction that their government had acted wisely, especially because the competing socialist system in the Soviet Union was in collapse at the same time. The West had been directed towards a course of deficits, a course of society fragmentation, and a course of inertia towards sociological and environmental problems. Sadly, the consequences of this move were slow in emerging. During the Reagan administration the accumulated debt of the US grew from 930 billion dollars to 2.7 trillion, or from 32% of GDP to 53% of GDP.

The tax increases introduced (against all the votes of the Republican Party in Congress) by the Clinton administration in 1993 halted and reversed this trend, but only temporarily.

When George W. Bush became president, his primary objective was a renewed reduction of taxes favouring the wealthy. In combination with two expensive wars and the financial crash of 2008 this inflated the federal debt to 10.7 trillion dollars (or 74 % of GDP) by the end of the Bush administration. In the years since then the administration of Barack Obama has failed to deal effectively with this problem, to a large extent because the economy is weak and because the Republican-controlled congress has been ideologically opposed to any kind of tax increase. The financial stratification of the US society (i.e., the concentration of wealth among the ultra-rich) is now more pronounced than it has ever been.

The generation which is presently in their productive years (30 to 55 years old), and you, the class of 2030, are the ones who suffer now and will suffer the most in the future from these shortfalls. In the long run, the debt will have to be paid for by inflation or ever more severe service cuts. In other words, all of you will pay for the greed of the generations which voted for the Reagan-Bush tax cuts.

2.2.2   A case study: California

California used to be the envy of the world. A place in the sun with apparently limitless resources and space, and a standard of living above anything else in the rest of the world. The golden state had it all: a productive bread basket in the central valley, industries (cars, planes, movies, computers, software) that were always cutting edge, thriving real estate markets, an educated work force. The state ran comfortable surplusses from property, state and sales taxes, and recycled this money into excellent schools, police and firefighting forces, state universities, and so on. The University of California system was one of the wealthiest and best public education systems in the world, a place where cutting edge research was done in almost any subject, and where higher education was the best available anywhere.

The California constitution allows a version of direct democracy which is rare elsewhere. Private initiatives can become law by collecting sufficiently many signatures and taking an issue to a public vote, after which it must become a law. In essence, this happened with what is now known as Proposition 13 (or, as it is properly called, "People's Initiative to Limit Property Taxation"). It was a successful drive to limit property taxes. I will describe its essence and effects in detail, but first, digest this: Should any state give its people the power to vote about whether and how much taxes they should pay? Taken to the extreme, citizens would certainly opt out of paying taxes, and would thus deprive their government from providing the services citizens expect from their government, like schools and teachers, roads with maintenance, police forces, and so on.

This is what Proposition 13 has effectively done to California. It was approved by voters on June 6, 1978 and is now embodied in Article 13A of the Constitution of the State of California [9]. Its very first paragraph limits the tax rate for real estate:

"The maximum amount of any ad valorem tax on real property shall not exceed one percent (1%) of the full cash value of such property. The one percent (1%) tax is to be collected by the counties and apportioned according to law to the districts within the counties."

The proposition decreased property taxes by assessing property values at their 1975 value and restricted annual increases of assessed value of real property to an inflation factor, not to exceed 2% per year. It prohibited reassessment of a new base year value except for (a) change in ownership or (b) completion of new construction.

The initiative further contained statements requiring a two-thirds majority in both legislative houses for future increases of any state tax rates or amounts of revenue collected, including income tax rates. It also requires a two-thirds vote majority in local elections for local governments wishing to increase special taxes.

A large contributor to the emergence and "success" of Proposition 13 was the sentiment that older Californians should not be priced out of their homes through high taxes. It is therefore no surprise that the aging middle class largely supported the proposition and helped its passage. Seniors with limited means should certainly not be taxed out of their homes, and other societies deal with this problem in other ways (for example, where I live seniors receive a reduction, called a homeowners grant, to alleviate their tax bill). The California idea was much more universal, and, as will be shown below, has had catastrophic consequences.

It has been estimated that Proposition 13 saved California homeowners some 528 billion dollars in taxes between 1978 and 2009. This money would have gone to fund schools, pay teacher's salaries, build and fix roads and other infrastructure, provide public pools, pay for prisons. The list is very long, and the necessary cash flow dried up with the passage of Proposition 13. As a consequence, California localities had to seek voters' approval for special assessments that would levy new taxes and fees for services that used to be paid for entirely or partially from property taxes: streets, water, sewer, electricity, infrastructure, schools, parks, police protection, firefighting units, penitentiary facilities. Sales tax rates increased from 6% (pre-Prop 13 level) to 8.25%.

California public schools were ranked nationally as among the best during the 1960s. By 2012 they had decreased to 48th place in many surveys of student achievement. Spending per pupil remained at the national average until about 1985, when it was forced into decline. This resulted in another referendum, Proposition 98, which directs a certain percentage of the state's budget towards education.

In 1978 California posted a budget surplus in excess of 5.5 billion (this was actually a factor leading to Proposition 13; homeowners argued that they were being taxed unnecessarily). In the fiscal year 2011-2012, California faced a shortfall of roughly 25 billion dollars. This after years of cutbacks which introduced unpaid furloughs for teachers, massive reductions of financial grants to universities (which in response have tripled tuition fees since 2001, laid off staff and cut salaries to make up for the shortfall), dramatic cutbacks in public works, and so forth. Public employees have been paid with IOUs. The spectre of state bankruptcy is now raised as a possibility, and some communities (Vallejo, Stockton [5]) have actually gone bankrupt because they could no longer meet their financial obligations.

A different but predictable side effect of Proposition 13 is that similar houses in the same neighbourhood can and do experience very different levels of taxation, especially in the wake of the housing bubble from 2000 to 2007. A house

that was assessed at \$ 100,000 in 1978, while unsold, could
for tax purposes not be assessed at more that \$ 190,000
in 2010. The same house, at the height of the housing
bubble in 2006, could have been sold at \$ 600,000, with a
proportionally higher assessment and tax bill. This built
in a massive inequity towards new home buyers, especially
younger families who were not in the market in 1978.

The proposition is sometimes called the "third rail"
(meaning "untouchable subject") of California politics, and
it is not popular politically for lawmakers to attempt to
change it. The class of 2030 in California, whose future
is being shaped in this state of affairs, is likely to face a
bleak reality: Public schools that are overcrowded and un-
derfunded, underpaid teachers, inadequate public services,
a dearth of jobs, a university system that is either in tatters
or unaffordable. The generational contract which used to
transfer the needed resources to the next generation was
cancelled in 1978. [4]

2.3   Destroying Capital: Wall Street and the Banking Industry

Karl Marx asserted that Capitalism produces more than
it consumes, and that capitalist societies will therefore engage in periodic destructions of capital. Historically, such
destructions happened in wars, or in particularly wasteful

---

[4]This section was first written in the late spring of 2012. Since then, there have
been renewed and genuine efforts in California to address the taxation issue. The
situation may turn around for the better.

consumer behaviours, such as long commutes in private vehicles with much demand on space and fuel (for example, in the city of Los Angeles, 70% of all space is dedicated to cars; this includes roads and parking spaces). Often, the destruction is led by the wealthy, while the consequences are disproportionately felt by the poor, very much in line with the Voltaire quote that *"the rich require an abundant supply of the poor."*

Periodically the middle class and the poor are deluded into promises of outrageous riches, by behaviours modelled for them by neighbours, friends, or the media. Stock markets are popular vehicles which channel such behaviours. The 1920s were a decade in the last century when unrestricted bank speculation made few people incredibly wealthy but drove many others into bankruptcy. The depression that followed the great crash of 1929 meant ruin and desperation for many who had been middle class just a few years earlier.

It was then realized that reckless speculation had the potential to not just bankrupt those who engaged in risky financial transactions, but to seriously damage the economy overall. To this end, laws were introduced to regulate some of the dangerous behaviours. This was a legacy of the Roosevelt administration which served America and the world well for 50 years.

First, the FDR administration introduced federal deposit insurance. The idea was to create consumer confidence and thus prevent runs on banks. The National Banking Act of 1933 (Glass-Steagall Act) separated commercial banking from investment banking, and it therefore sheltered most private savings from excessive risk. These regulations stayed in effect into the seventies, when they started to crumble under lobbying efforts by the financial industry.

Investment banking remained a niche market until 1987, when the Federal Reserve Bank permitted selected large banks to underwrite more risky securities. By 1999, all the legal restrictions imposed by the Glass-Steagall Act were removed. The softening and eventual rescinding of these regulations was accompanied by a recurrence of market crashes and speculative bubbles. We provide a short list. The details are easily found on the internet and nicely summarized in Wikipedia.

2.3.1   A short list of banking crises after deregulation

a) The Savings and Loan (S&L) Disaster

Financial deregulation starting in the 1970s and 1980s allowed ed S&Ls to enter risky financial domains, offering exceedingly complex products and lending imprudently large sums in direct competition with the major US commercial banks—but without the banks' expertise, and outside of the banks' strict regulatory framework. Many S&Ls soon found themselves in deep financial trouble. A run began first of all on S&L institutions in Ohio and Maryland in 1985. About 25% of America's 4,000-plus S&L's eventually went bankrupt. A US economic professor later referred to this as *"the largest and costliest venture in public misfeasance, malfeasance and larceny of all time"*. And because the federal government had insured many of the individual deposits in the S&Ls, it found itself facing a gigantic liability when they collapsed: the total cost of the bailout came to $150 bn.

b) Black Monday (October 19, 1987).

North American markets dropped by 22% in one day. The most popular explanation to date is computer program trading, which triggered knee-jerk reactions (and inflated selling) in response to an anticipated and overdue market correction. This crash corrected itself in a relatively short time. In this case no government intervention occurred.

c) The LTCM crash (Long-Term Capital Management; see en.wikipedia.org/wiki/Long-Term_Capital_Management)

Long-Term Capital Management L.P. (LTCM) was a speculative hedge fund based in Greenwich, Connecticut that utilized absolute-return trading strategies (fixed-income arbitrage, statistical arbitrage, and pairs trading) combined with high leverage. The firm's master hedge fund, Long-Term Capital Portfolio L.P., failed in the late 1990s, leading to a bailout by other financial institutions under the supervision of the New York Federal Reserve Bank.

LTCM was founded in 1994 by John Merriwether, the former vice-chairman and head of bond trading at Salomon Brothers. The Board of directors members included Myron Scholes and Robert C. Merton, who shared the 1997 Nobel Memorial Prize in Economic Sciences for a "new method to determine the value of derivatives". Initially successful with annualized returns of over 40% in its first years, in 1998 LTCM lost $4.6 billion in less than four months following a Russian financial crisis, requiring financial intervention by the New York Federal Reserve Bank. The fund closed in early 2000.

The key problem was that the fund had to take highly-leveraged positions to make a significant profit. Early in 1998 the firm had equity of $4.72 billion and had borrowed over $124.5 billion (with assets of around $129 billion), for a debt to equity ratio of over 25 to 1. It had off-balance sheet derivative positions with a notional value of approximately $1.25 trillion, most of which were in interest rate derivatives such as interest rate swaps. The fund also invested in other derivatives such as equity options. The highly-leveraged position multiplied gains and losses and thus produced inherent instability in LTCM's holdings, a dire precursor to the situation many financial institutions faced ten years later, during the great crash of 2008 (see below).

d) The Dot-Com bubble

The dot-com bubble (also referred to as the Internet bubble or the Information Technology Bubble) was a speculative bubble covering roughly the years 1995 to 2000 (a climax occurred on March 10, 2000, with the NASDAQ peaking at 5132.52 in intraday trading before closing at 5048.62) during which stock markets in industrialized nations saw their equity value rise rapidly from growth in the Internet sector and related fields. While the latter part was a boom and bust cycle, the Internet boom is sometimes meant to refer to the steady commercial growth of the Internet with the advent of the world wide web, as exemplified by the first release of the Mosaic web browser in 1993, and continuing through the 1990s. The period was marked by the founding (and often spectacular failure) of a family of new Internet-based companies commonly referred to as dot-coms. Companies were seeing their stock prices shoot up if they simply added an "e-" prefix to their name and/or a ".com" to the end, which one author called "prefix investing". A combination of rapidly increasing stock prices, market confidence that the companies would turn future profits, individual speculation in stocks, and widely available venture capital created an environment in which many investors were ready to overlook traditional metrics such as P/E ratio in favour of confidence in technological advancements.

The collapse of the bubble took place during 2000-2001. Many upstart companies, such as Pets.com, failed completely. Others lost a large portion of their market capitalization but remained stable and profitable, e.g., Cisco, whose stock declined by 86%. Some later recovered and surpassed their dot-com-bubble peaks, e.g., Amazon, whose stock went from 107 to 7 dollars per share, but sits at 253 dollars as I write this. Many communication companies were forced to file for bankruptcy. One of the more significant players, WorldCom, was found practicing illegal accounting practices to exaggerate its profits on a yearly basis. WorldCom's stock price fell drastically when this information went public, and it eventually filed the third-largest corporate bankruptcy in U.S. history. Other examples include NorthPoint Communications, Global Crossing, JDS Uniphase, XO Communications, and Covad Communications. Companies such as Nortel, Cisco and Corning were at a disadvantage because they bet on infrastructure that was never developed, and their sales dropped accordingly. The stock price of Nortel peaked at $ 124.00 (at which point Nortel made up about a third of the Toronto stock index) and eventually dropped to under $ 0.50. The company stock is no longer trading at the present time. Millions of investors lost a large fraction of their savings.

e) The Housing bubble (2001-2007)

After the collapse of the dot-com bubble, subsequent lowering of interest rates as set by the Federal Reserve Bank under the "blind" leadership of Alan Greenspan encouraged more and more Americans (and soon the English, Spaniards, Irishmen, ...) to borrow large sums of money and invest in real estate. This resulted in rapidly increasing valuation for real estate, and prices in the sunshine states of California, Nevada, Arizona and Florida doubled within a few short years. Amazingly, there were many who assumed that this was healthy and sustainable. David Lereah, former chief economist of the National Association of Realtors (NAR), distributed "Anti-Bubble Reports" in August 2005 to "respond to the irresponsible bubble accusations made by your local media and local academics." Among other statements, these reports stated that people "should [not] be concerned that home prices are rising faster than family income", that "there is virtually no risk of a national housing price bubble based on the fundamental demand for housing and predictable economic factors", and that "a general slowing in the rate of price growth can be expected, but in many areas inventory shortages will persist and home prices are likely to continue to rise above historic norms."

We know the outcome of such thinking. Prices rose to ridiculous levels, and at the same time the deregulated markets found ways to provide even those with marginal incomes with credit (sub-prime mortgages). This led directly to

f) The financial crisis of 2008.

Much has been written about this financial calamity, so I will leave it here with a brief summary. The housing bubble from 2001-2007 was a classic example of a Ponzi scheme, although at the time most people failed to realize this, and many others simply were in denial. There were, of course, a few intelligent warning voices, but they were not listened to or even laughed at by politicians and bankers alike. Too much money was being made easily by borrowing against imagined future astronomical gains in home values.

Credit was cheap and abundantly provided by the incompetent leadership of Alan Greenspan and the Federal Reserve Bank. People with low incomes and poor credit had access to subprime mortgages, offered by the tens of thousands by specialized financial institutions (New Century, Countrywide Financial, and many others: who can remem-

ber them now, a scant five years later). The debts, most
of which were unlikely to ever be paid off, were then bun-
dled in financial packages called collateralized debt obligations (CDOs) and traded by Wall Street investment banks.
This business created secondary financial products which
became known as credit default swaps (CDSs), effectively
insurance contracts on CDOs; The CDS business led to
the creation of synthetic CDOs (replicas of the original
CDOs, which could simply be insured many times over).
All the big Wall Street banks and many foreign players (famously in Iceland, Germany, France, the United Kingdom,
Japan and Switzerland) engaged in this business, usually
with borrowed money, and frequently with huge leverage.
When Bear Stearns became the first Wall Street investment
bank to face bankruptcy in March 2008, they were lever-
aged at 35:1. Bear Stearns avoided bankruptcy by letting
itself be absorbed by JP Morgan. Its stock price dropped
from 172 dollars in January 2007 to 2 dollars at the time of
the takeover.

In September 2008 matters came to a head: The insurance giant AIG and the investment banks Lehman Brothers
and Merrill Lynch all faced bankruptcy at about the same
time. Lehman really went bankrupt; AIG was rescued by
the government with many billions of tax dollars; Bank of
America was coerced into absorbing Merrill Lynch, and its
finances (and stock price) have reflected this calamity ever
since. Of the large Wall Street investment banks, Goldman
Sachs, Morgan Stanley and JP Morgan survived. Eventually, the US government pumped 700 billion dollars into

the banking system to prevent further collapse, a program which became known as TARP (Troubled Assets Relief Program). While this saved the system, millions of people who had participated in the Ponzi scheme lost their houses to foreclosure, millions of others lost all or a large fraction of their investments, and the inevitable recession cost many their jobs. Government debts skyrocketed. The recession has still not ended as I write this.

It is very difficult to produce an estimate of the cumulative losses of these crises. The first three, while producing losses amounting to hundreds of billions to individuals and governments, seem puny in comparison to the latter three. The dot-com bubble, the housing bubble and the financial crisis of 2008 caused private and public losses amounting to many trillions of dollars, the same order of magnitude as the accumulated federal debt of the U.S. There was no compelling reason why these losses had to occur; they could have been avoided had reason and regulation prevailed. What did prevail were greed and speculation, and the wasted money will be missing in your legacy, class of 2030.

2.3.2 Who will pay the bill?

You will by now have realized that the destroyed capital should have been yours, to finance your needs in the general sense. As I write this, governments around the world are cutting programs in efforts to balance budgets; however, what they cannot cut are the interest costs for the ever growing deficits and accumulated debts. The traditional way out of this mess is for governments to either devalue their currency, or, if that is not an option (as in the currently troubled economies of Greece, Portugal, Italy and Spain), by implementing draconian austerity measures. History suggests inflation as a remedy, for example, by printing money (that way, everybody gets a little poorer; the wealthy, of course, have the option to invest their riches into resources which tend to keep their value, like land, gold, or oil).

The total accumulated debt in the US is at present roughly 50 trillion dollars, or about 3.5 times GDP. This includes federal debt, state and communal debts, and personal debts.

Private US citizens, who typically sit on mountains of personal debt (mortgage debt, consumer loans or credit card debt), now owe on average 126% of a year's income. In Canada, the corresponding figure is 150%. Debt is the bulk of the legacy we leave for future generations.

Many years ago, Thomas Jefferson issued a dire warning about banks and debt:

"If the American people ever allow the banks to control the issuance of their currency, first by inflation and then by deflation, the banks and corporations that will grow up around them will deprive the people of all property until their children will wake up homeless. I sincerely believe the banking institutions (having the issuing power of money) are more dangerous to liberty than standing armies. My zeal against these institutions was so warm and open at the

establishment of the Bank of the United States (Hamilton's foreign system), that I was derided as a maniac by the tribe of bank mongers who were seeking to filch from the public."

Clearly, Jefferson had little faith in the leadership provided by banks. At the present time, for better or for worse, banks hold a disproportionate amount of influence and power, even those on the verge of bankruptcy, because of their sheer size.

Chapter 3

Broken Contracts

3.1 Education, only for the Rich

In the middle ages education was a privilege of the aristocracy, the clergy, and the rich. The clergy provided lessons in reading, writing, history and religious education, moulding their pupils towards the generally accepted model of society: power, wealth and education for the all powerful ruling class, shared with the wealth and controlling spiritual domination of the clergy. Poor peasants lived in ignorance and illiteracy, and were kept hoping for a better life in heaven, a prospect promised in return for "good" behaviour in this life. They toiled, starved, fought wars for their masters, and listened to their priests. Information in the form of written material was only available to the few literate, and you could only become literate by serving the system in one way or the other, either by joining the clergy, or by obtaining a position in the service of your government.

It was Martin Luther who in 1524 first called for the

establishment of "Christian schools" for all boys and girls, and in 1592 the district Pfalz-Zweibrücken in Germany became the first in the world to introduce obligatory school attendance. Strasbourg followed in 1598. The enlightenment and the subsequent industrial revolution in the 18th and 19th centuries prepared society and created a need for a better educated population, and forward-thinking politicians and monarchs (like Friedrich II of Prussia) furthered the establishment and support of schools and universities. *"Upon the education of the people the fate of this country depends,"* said Benjamin Disraeli famously in the 19th century. His words now apply to all countries and societies.

Education of the young is a long-term investment. My own education started at age 6 and ended, with a Ph.D., at age 26. I attended primary school for four years, then high school for another 9 years, then 4 years of university in Heidelberg, then another 3 years in Berkeley and Bonn towards the Ph.D. And, of course, my parents supported me for 17 of these 20 years, although I did cover part of my expenses while studying in Heidelberg as a teaching assistant. I remember that when I first entered high school, there was still a monthly fee (called "Schulgeld"), some 20 marks or so per month, a significant amount of money in 1960. After a year or so this fee was discontinued—it was recognized as discrimination against the poor, and the government abandoned it. And I entered the university of Heidelberg in the famous year of unrest, 1968. Again, there were some (very modest) student fees to be paid, which I did pay for one term before these fees were abolished, too.

Of course, this did not mean that access to high school and university were universal. You had to meet admission standards by reaching a certain grade point average in an already rather selective high school system. In fact, in 1960 only 6% of German youths entered university at all (most of the others left the school system at various possible exit points and entered the country's well developed apprenticeship program). Over the years, this figure has risen dramatically, and the system has really changed rather a lot. But I digress.

The point is that in, say, 1970, school education and university access in the first and second worlds were wide open to those who had the needed intellect. It is true that in the advanced education institutions of the United States and many other countries there were tuition fees, but these were of an order of magnitude which allowed your family to afford the financial sacrifice, and/or you could finance your studies by working on the side, or taking on a modest loan. The bulk of the cost of your education was covered by the state, say, by tax money. The state was willing to make this investment because well educated citizens were a recipe for better productivity in the future.

So here is what happened next, class of 2030. Really, there were two parallel developments, which reinforced each other. Let's talk about schools first.

First, there had always been private schools you could attend if you could afford the extra high tuition and/ or boarding costs. These schools had the advantage that you could usually be admitted even if your grade point average was low, and children of the wealthy had traditionally used this avenue if other schools were closed to them due to a substandard grade point average. Clearly, there would be few children from poorer neighbourhoods, or poorer minorities, to share the classroom with.

Second, due to the tax "revolution" we discussed in the previous sections, funding for the public school systems began to dry up. Teachers' salaries were frozen or cut (for example, by "furloughs," unpaid vacations which amounted to something like a 10% salary cut), class sizes increased, and nonessential programs like Music, Theatre, Sports, etc. were more and more neglected. Of course, this resulted in more people with means and influence sending their children to private schools, then craving for more tax cuts, thus exacerbating the funding crisis, etc. You see the vicious cycle.

At the University level things are more complex. Leading private universities (Harvard, Stanford, Princeton, Cornell and others in an elite list) are largely immune—they will take those who are smart enough and can afford it, and they will sponsor the bright students who cannot afford it. These universities also sit on gigantic endowments. Problems arise with schools (Universities and colleges) that depend on public money and are the prime destinations for those who are average students: not good or wealthy enough to get into Stanford, but certainly qualified for a degree. The University of California system and the California State Universities are cases in point.

Tuition at Berkeley for in-state students was about $

4,500.00 per year in 1998. For 2012, it was listed at over $ 15,000.00 (I mentioned before that University tuition costs have tripled). Similar ratios hold elsewhere, except that tuition costs are typically larger. Emory University in Atlanta, Georgia, quotes tuition costs in excess of $ 30,000.00 per year (of course, this is to be augmented by living expenses, and you can expect to need $ 50,000.00 per year, or in excess of $ 200,000.00 for a four-year program).

Some students win scholarships to mitigate these costs. Others work on the side (though it is all but impossible to finance such expenses by a part-time job). Some students have wealthy parents (but we are not writing about this part of society). Many take on student loans and end up with crushing debt upon graduation. Imagine you are 24 years old, have just graduated with, say, a business or English degree from a good university, hold $ 180,000.00 in student loans, and you cannot find a decently paying job for years. This is no longer a hypothetical scenario, it is (and will become more so) the reality for many university graduates.

Of course, even these increased tuition fees are not sufficient to really finance the university system. Cuts, direct or indirect, have to be made in other ways— increased class sizes, cuts in programs, libraries and other services. Retiring faculty are often not replaced, and the workload is redistributed to the remaining colleagues, who find ever more stress and less satisfaction in their jobs. As I write sitting at a Canadian University desk, this sad reality is all around me.

If we extrapolate for 18 years, you are likely to live in a household that has trouble meeting its financial obligations. You have gone through a school curriculum that has been severely compromised in order to accommodate cutbacks that became necessary due to tax cuts. You face a university education which will put you hundreds of thousands of dollars in the hole, with uncertain job prospects upon graduation.

The cumulative effect of these developments, put together, will be an unhealthy and dangerous stratification of society, mostly at the expense of the middle class. More and more wealth is concentrating in the richest 1% (or 5%) of society, while the lower middle class is being pushed towards the margins of poverty because of the mismatch between their eroding earnings and growing debts. The predictable (and observed) effect will be a fractured and largely dysfunctional society, in which the well-to-do will isolate themselves from the rest of society, while large sections of this same society are essentially abandoned. This is going to happen at many levels, from physical separation as enforced by the concept of a gated community, to separation in medical care, as enforced by price, to separation by education and job prospects. It will be almost like in the middle ages, where nobility lived in castles, conscripted and taxed the peasants but had otherwise little obligation towards them. We discuss some of the current symptoms in the next section.

3.2 The fractured society

A utopian society is one in which all age and society groups co-operate and share knowledge, production capacities and facilities to the advantage of all. This was the ideal of communism, and we know that it did not work. Human nature is not consistent with the ideal. Still, the concept of social democratic societies, launched in the 19th century and realized in many societies in the 20th, translated the idealistic ideas into reality to a large degree: Generational contracts would provide universal education to the young and health and pension benefits to the old; taxation would take some of the profits and wages of the financially most successful and use them to provide services for all; legislation would curtail behaviours which threaten such contracts.

I related in previous chapters how neoconservative efforts have already damaged this social democratic model. Here, I wish to talk about a phenomenon which is a physical manifestation of the consequences of these developments: the gated community.

The class of 2030 will be split not just into those few who come from the wealthiest 5%, or the shrunken upper middle class, and the rest, but also into those who grew up in protected, sheltered communities which are "gated", i.e., separated from the rest of the community by guards and walls, and the rest. The gated community is something like a reverse prison—the idea is to keep everybody else out. Gated communities thrive especially in countries which have particularly strong stratification in society wealth and (or) high crime rates; it is obvious that abundance of the poor and high crime rates are connected. For these reasons, gated communities are common in Brazil, Mexico, India, Russia, South Africa and Nigeria. The security motivation is also a strong factor for the creation of gated communities in the United States, where such enclaves abound in Florida, California and the desert states (or, more generally, the sun belt). These latter communities target especially wealthy retirees, and some (so-called "adult" communities) explicitly exclude children and teenagers. It is expensive to move into such communities, and ironic that tax cuts are called for and provided by conservative governments, while the savings of the taxpayer are then reinvested in this type of isolation from the outside world.

Here are some excerpts of what you can find on the internet about the subject:

"the most common form of gated community in Brazil is called "condominio fechado" (closed housing estate) and is the object of desire of the upper classes. A closed housing estate is a small town with its own infrastructure (backup power supply, sanitation, security guards). The purpose of such a community is protection of its residents from outside violence."

"In Argentina, gated communities are often seen as a symbol of wealth but enjoy dubious social prestige. While most gated communities have only houses, some bigger ones have their own hospital, school, shopping mall, and more. In recent years, this influx of people going from the big cities to the gated communities has experienced a backlash in Argentina. Visiting Buenos Aires, the renowned geographer and urbanist Jordi Borja (from Spain) who teaches urban planning at the University of Barcelona criticized gated communities, calling them *the negation of cities* . Architect and university professor Marcela Camblor, who heads the Urban Design Dept in Florida, told the La Nacion newspaper that "the gated communities experiment has failed", calling them "unsustainable from the economic, social, and now even energetic point of view".

"In post-apartheid South Africa, gated communities have mushroomed in response to high levels of violent crime. South African gated communities are broadly classified as "security villages" (large-scale privately developed areas) or "enclosed" neighbourhoods. Some of the newest neighbourhoods being developed are almost entirely composed of security villages, with a few isolated malls and other essential services (such as hospitals). A common mode of development of the security villages involves staking out a large land claim, building a high wall surrounding the entire zone, then gradually adding roads and other infrastructure. In part, property developers have adopted this response to counter squatting, which local residents fear due to associated crime, and which often results in a protracted eviction process."'

"In Saudi Arabia, gated communities have existed since the discovery of oil, mainly to accommodate Westerners and their families."

"Mexico has both the largest population of gated community dwellers in the world and the largest number of

gated community dwellers as a percentage of national population. It is estimated that there are 56.8 million Mexicans
living in gated communities as of 2010. Gated communities in Mexico are a result of the huge income gap existing
in the country. A 2008 study found that the average income in an urban area of Mexico was $26,654, a rate higher
than advanced nations like South Korea or Taiwan, while
the average income in rural areas (sometimes just miles
away) was only $8,403. This close a proximity of wealth
and poverty has created a large perceived security risk for
Mexico's middle class. Gated communities can be found in
virtually every medium and large size city in Mexico with
the largest found in major cities, such as Monterrey, Mexico
City or Guadalajara."

"In the US, ... by 1997, an estimated 20,000 gated communities had been built across the country. Approximately
40% of new homes in California are behind walls. In 1997,
estimates of the number of people in gated communities
ranged from 4 million in 30,000 communities up to around
8 million, with 0.5 million in California alone. It is difficult
to determine how many gated communities there are in the
United States because most are privately developed."

Europe has very few gated communities.

Let us think this through. People move behind walls,
and in some cases behind electrified fences, in order to protect themselves from crime, pollution, traffic, urban decay,
and poverty. They pay extra for this advantage. They can
leave at will, but only through the official gates. They can
invite guests to come and visit and share the many avail-

able amenities like swimming pools, tennis courts, entertainment, etc. It all sounds good. So what is the problem?

The concept of a gated community fractures society physically and psychologically; Services are split between "in" and "out". The walls and fences fracture the landscape and the population into domains where you can or cannot go, imposing severe restrictions on people's freedom to visit, explore and experience other parts of their world. Those living "outside" are kept outside (which is the main point of a gated community), but those on the inside also have access only to "their" inside, not to other gated communities except by invitation. This is the antithesis of the idea of free movement or travel.

Chapter 4

Depletion. As fast as possible?

4.1 Of Oil Sands and Pipelines

I live in Canada. Apart from the weather, which can drive you crazy in most parts of the country at various times of the year, this is certainly one of the best countries in the world to live in. Its vast expanse gives us a feeling of freedom and security; its gigantic resources promise untold wealth for many generations; its educated people and work force augur stability and prosperity, perpetual and solid democratic institutions, excellent health and social benefits.

However, not all is rosy in our golden realm of the north. Subversion of democracy as discussed in Chapter 2 is at work here, too. To begin with, we have a poor, obsolete electoral system, in which the "first past the post" electoral candidate in any particular riding gets to sit in parliament. In a system with many parties, this produces results which can be far from proportional representation, will say, a party which garnered only 40 % of all votes may hold a solid majority in parliament.

This is exactly what happened in the federal election of 2011. There were then and are now 5 major parties in Canada: Conservative, Liberal, New Democratic Party, Green, and the Bloc Quebecois (which runs only in Quebec). Vote-splitting between the Liberal, NDP and Green parties produced a conservative majority government, elected by a minority of the people (a minority of those who voted).

This government has become known as the Harper government, because it is very much driven by the person and agenda of Prime Minister Stephen Harper. Harper is in charge for roughly four years, and it appears that his government is using their power to push for the interests of those who are the prime supporters of their philosophy, namely, the business interests of the oil and gas industry which is mostly based in Alberta. This agenda is pushed forward in a relentless fashion, often against the will of the majority of Canadians, and in ways which border on abuse of power.

The new style has been referred to as "bullying" [12], and indeed, scientists/ academics/ publicists who question the agenda face official "muzzling", i.e., their free expression of opinions and free exchange of ideas with the media is discouraged to the point of real or threatened dismissals from government jobs. Laws which "hinder" the business interests are changed without proper procedure or inquiry, and opponents are denigrated in negative ads or public interviews.

This last type of behaviour is particularly true with respect to environmental issues, and is best illustrated by an important and current example. At this particular time, the oil industry, with the uncritical support of the Harper government, is planning a big pipeline, known as "The Northern Gateway Pipeline", and proposed by the Calgary pipeline giant Enbridge Inc. This pipeline will connect the oil fields of northern Alberta with the Pacific port of Kitimat, a distance of roughly 1,200 km, and will cross many hundreds of waterways. The pipeline will largely pass through wilderness, partly Crown land and partly land owned by the First Nations. At the terminus the oil is to be loaded into tankers destined for the vibrant economies of the Asian Pacific Rim. In the summer of 2012, the pipeline project was a daily news item in western Canada, and there was and is massive opposition by environmental groups, the First Nations, and business interests which profit from the tourism and fishing industries.

Let us listen what Prime Minister Stephen Harper had to say on the CBC news in January 2012, faced with criticism of the project.

"Just because certain people in the United States would like to see Canada be one giant national park for the northern half of North America, I don't think that's part of what our review process is all about. Our process is there to determine what the needs and desires of Canadians are."

Harper was implying here that opposition to the project

was foreign-based; he conveniently ignored the massive opposition inside Canada, especially in British Columbia, whose territory the pipeline would cross. He also chose to ignore the massive foreign interests *in support* of this pipeline, like Chinese oil companies, or foreign investment in the oil sands as those of the American tycoons David and Charles Koch (see [3]).

In an open letter, Natural Resources Minister Joe Oliver wrote

"Unfortunately, there are environmental and other radical groups that would seek to block this opportunity to diversify our trade."

The implication here is that environmentalists trying to prevent the pipeline are radicals opposed to free trade. Or what else is Oliver trying to say? He continued:

"Their goal is to stop any major project no matter what the cost to Canadian families in lost jobs and economic growth. No forestry. No mining. No oil. No gas. No more hydro-electric dams. They ... threaten to hijack our regulatory system to achieve their radical ideological agenda, stack the hearings with people to delay or kill good projects, attract "jet-setting" celebrities and use funding from foreign special interest groups."

It was immediately clear from these comments that the Harper government wanted that pipeline. Opponents were drawn as radicals, enemies of any technological progress, or agents of foreign interests. A shameful conduct, unworthy of an elected official.

Let us explore the background. At this time, Canada has the second largest proven oil reserves in the world (next to Saudi Arabia). Most of this oil is deposited in a shallow form as oil sands which are expensive, wasteful and polluting to extract. The oil is retrieved by open-pit mining, and then extracted from the "sand" with heat and hot water. The water and energy requirements for this are gigantic. Large landmasses are effectively turned into a wasteland (hopefully, to be eventually recovered as forest land), and there are massive amounts of greenhouse gas emissions and water pollution. The process is economically viable while oil is sufficiently expensive and while enough energy is cheaply available for the extraction process. Needless to say, it's controversial from an environmental point of view.

Alberta, BC and Saskatchewan also hold large reserves of natural gas, some of which is presently used to extract oil. Ironically, a comparatively clean source of energy (the gas) is used to extract a rather "dirty" source of energy (the oil). It adds up at the bank because gas is cheap and oil is expensive. The conventional proven gas reserves would only last 10 years at present rate of use.

A related and also controversial issue is the exploration for and exploitation of gas reserves held in shale formations, gas reserves which can be tapped with the fairly new technology of "hydraulic fracturing" (or, short, "fracking"). The potential gas reserves to be retrieved by this practice are not known but clearly huge. However, fracking also is a highly controversial practice because of the dangers of ground water contamination and subsoil collapses, which can lead to earthquakes. Caution is certainly advisable. Some states in the U.S. have made fracking illegal (Vermont), while others have embraced it whole-heartedly (North Dakota).

Let us get back to the Enbridge Northern Gateway Pipeline. Its environmental risks are immediately clear: There is the potential for oil leaks along the route, with all the cultural, economic and environmental implications for the local people, and for the streams and creeks which stand to be contaminated. One might think that this risk is small and would be localized, but unfortunately, Enbridge has a terrible safety record for its pipelines. As I write this, they have just been slammed in a review by the U.S. National Transportation Safety Board (NTSB) regarding a spill in Michigan, in which more than 3 million litres of oil leaked into wetlands, Talmadge Creek and the Kalamazoo River, after a pipeline belonging to Enbridge ruptured near Marshall, Mich., on July 25, 2010. A worker from a local gas utility reported the spill to Enbridge's control centre 17 hours and 19 minutes after the line had failed, and after repeatedly ignoring warning signs and reports of a spill.

In its report, the NTSB said that not only was Enbridge's response to the spill slow, but the company knew at least five years before the massive leak that the pipeline was corroded and cracked. External corrosion and cracking caused the 471-kilometre pipeline to rupture, the NTSB said. A presenter at the hearing stated that roughly 15,000 defects were identified in a 2005 report. About 900 of those were dug up, and it was noted that the one that spilled was not among those tapped for digging. [11]. The company expects to spend $ 765 million cleaning up — five times more than the next costliest onshore cleanup effort—with its insurance footing most of the bill.

Here is what Enbridge CEO, Patrick D. Daniel, had to say to that: *"We very much appreciate the patience of residents in the communities who were affected by the Line 6B release. Under the direction of the U.S. Environmental Protection Agency and local health authorities, the Kalamazoo River was re-opened last month for recreational use. We are also pleased to note that wildlife has returned to the area. We believe that the experienced personnel involved in the decisions made at the time of the release were trying to do the right thing. As with most such incidents, a series of unfortunate events and circumstances resulted in an outcome no one wanted."*

The word apology was not mentioned.

It is also informative to read what Stephen J. Wuori, president, Liquids Pipelines at Enbridge had to contribute: *"Safety has always been core to our operations. Our intent from the beginning of this incident has been to learn from it so we can prevent it from happening again, and to also share what we have learned with other pipeline operators. Enbridge and [Enbridge Energy Partners L.P.] conducted a detailed internal investigation of this incident in the months following the release and have made numerous enhancements to their processes, procedures and training as a result of the findings of the investigation, including in the control centre. Incident prevention, detection and re-*

sponse have also been enhanced. We will carefully examine the findings in the NTSB report to determine whether any further adjustments are appropriate."

Note the absence of anything specific in the meaningless drawl. And since these events and statements there has been another spill from an Enbridge pipeline, this time in Wisconsin. Regrettably, pipeline spills are not isolated incidents—they appear to happen with disturbing frequency.

The Federal Government in Ottawa and the provincial governments in Alberta and BC at first treated these news with silence. It appears that they were counting on the short memory of the public. When the public would not quiet down, the BC Liberal government under its leadership of Christy Clark waded in, starting a fight with its Alberta counterpart not about the project itself, but rather about how to share the expected revenues. And Stephen Harper himself broke his silence in August 2012, stating that the decision about the pipeline would be based on scientific inquiry; what he meant by that is open to interpretation, but given his treatment of scientists in other domains, one must assume that he was thinking of an economic analysis. Fair enough; but the results of an economic analysis depend very much on the variables you enter into it—if you only compute short-term revenues, you are likely to come out with the result Harper wants. If you give the environment and its long-term health a value, and you include the benefits and risks for future generations, you may get a very different result. Economics, sorry to say, is not an exact science.

Let us get back to safety issues related to the pipeline. It is hard to believe, but accidents with the pipeline are actually the *smaller* of two big dangers related to the project. The bigger danger is the risk of a supertanker calamity akin to the notorious Exxon Valdez disaster in Alaska (1989). At the rate at which Enbridge plans to pump heavy oil to the coast, an order of magnitude of 200 supertankers a year will have to navigate the narrow fjords of northern BC towards the open Pacific Ocean. A massive oil spill is not just likely; it is only a question of "When" and will cause untold environmental and economic damage to the northern BC Coast and its fishery and tourism potential.

Finally, rapid exploitation of the oil sands is also questionable from an economic point of view (this brings us back to economics). The only reason why the oil sands should be dug up as fast as planned is increased short-term profit for the involved companies (and, for that matter, the derived royalties for the Federal and Alberta governments). All other economic considerations point towards a slow, careful pace in exploiting this resource—oil and gas reserves are not just important fuels, they are also valuable raw materials for the chemical industry, and are to gain in value as world supplies decline. An argument can be made that a barrel of oil left in the ground will grow faster in value than the dollars it could be sold for today. Slow recovery of the oil will also reduce the greenhouse gas emissions and help to alleviate climate change (a topic we visit in the next section).

Thomas Mulcair, present leader of the NDP, the official party of opposition in Ottawa, has argued that aggressive mining of these energy resources pushes up the value of the Canadian dollar (turning it into a petrodollar) and thereby negatively affects export-oriented manufacturing in Canada (mostly in Ontario and Quebec). He referred to this as "Dutch" disease and was promptly and severely criticized by the Harper and Alberta governments for the comment. However, for the class of 2030, a vibrant and sustained manufacturing sector is a lot more relevant than rapid exploitation of a non-renewable resource in 2012. And you have a vital interest in avoiding serious environmental damage from both a local and global point of view. It is really rather trivial: Rather than invest in the future (your future) the present government is pushing an agenda that will sell Canadian oil and gas at an accelerating rate, with short-term profits the main objective.

4.2   Climate change

You live in world where the CO_2 content in the atmosphere stand in excess of 430 ppm (as I write this, in June 2012, it is 397 ppm, and rising by about 2 ppm every year). Scientists have warned for many years now that this man-made change of the atmosphere is a very dangerous phenomenon, with likely irreversible consequences. Here is a short list:

- The (observed) global warming, which is most reasonably explained by the greenhouse effect caused by these enhanced levels of CO_2, causes melting of glaciers and icecaps. Such melting is already widely observed as I write this. Among the consequences will be water shortages (or, temporarily, flooding) in areas which depend on glacial runoff, and

- An expected rise in the ocean levels, with flooding of low-lying areas like the Netherlands, Florida, Bangladesh, and many others.

- Vanishing of permafrost in the subarctic landmass. This is happening and widely documented.

- Ocean acidification. This is an effect which is not directly related to climate change, but may by itself be the most disastrous of all the consequences of the saturation with CO_2. Much of the CO_2 is absorbed from the atmosphere into the oceans. This, by itself, might not be a problem, as the oceans already hold the unimaginable amount of 36,000 gt (gigatons) of the gas (the total anthropocentric CO_2 emissions amount to an order of magnitude of 30 gt per year). The trouble is that the absorbed gas stays in the upper layers of the ocean (the top 400 meters or so) for millennia, and this is exactly the part of the ocean which is the ecosphere for coral reefs, plankton, shellfish, and in fact of much of the maritime food chain. The acidification of this layer is likely to do untold damage to these organisms. Signs of stress are already widely observed.

- Extreme weather. This includes long, persistent and devastating droughts and/ or floods. Australia saw both in recent years. Texas saw its worst drought ever in 2011. Hurricanes and Tornadoes appear to be both more frequent and stronger than historical records suggest. In this year, 2012, the U.S. has experienced its worst drought in 80 years, and the mid-Atlantic coast was hit and devastated by Hurricane "Sandy", which caused some $ 50 billion in damages. Increased food prices are predicted as a consequence of the persistent drought conditions. The combined effects of mega-droughts and glacial melts are already leading to conflicts regarding water supplies, especially in the Middle East and South Asia.

It would be possible for the generation which is presently in charge to address the CO_2 emission problem, and there are honest efforts by scientists and politicians alike. The challenge is to make the transition from a world economy based on fossil fuel consumption to one based on non-polluting renewable energy sources. This is a challenge to all societies and political leaders. Regrettably, there is not only hesitation; there are political leaders who flatly deny that there is a problem and accuse concerned scientists of corruption. Here is what Rick Perry, governor of Texas and briefly a contender for the Republican presidential nomination, said in the fall of 2011 (his language is left verbatim):

"I do believe that the issue of global warming has been politicized. I think there are a substantial number of sci-

entists who have manipulated data so that they will have dollars rolling into their projects. I think we are seeing it almost weekly or even daily, scientists who are coming forward and questioning the original idea that man-made global warming is what is causing the climate to change. Yes, our climates change. They have been changing ever since the earth was formed."

Perry's reasoning is consistent with the inaction shown by the previous GOP president, George W. Bush, who was very much a supporter of the oil and gas industry (his Vice President Dick Cheney was directly involved) and behaved as if concerned scientists were enemies of America.

Here are some of the standard arguments raised by the climate-change-denial industry.

First, some deniers even question whether humans are actually responsible for the CO_2 rise. After all, there is geological evidence that millions of years ago, when no human occupied the planet, CO_2 levels were at times much higher than now. The argument is that the rise could have natural origins, though these origins are usually not explained. And in any case, this argument fails to explain what would otherwise happen with the (undeniable) 30 gt we do emit every year. Simple math suggests that the rise in atmospheric CO_2 is exactly what you would expect if you had the anthropogenic emissions we produce (there are larger emissions in the natural biosphere, on the order of 750 gt every year, but the natural absorptions are of this same order; hence the very stable level of CO_2 seen over millennia until the industrial revolution in the 18th century began to disturb this balance.) A very clean and convincing discussion of the process can be found in [10].

A second argument concedes that anthropogenic emissions are the cause but that the rise in CO_2 does not matter, or is even beneficial. There are arguments about feedback mechanisms that will actually prevent disastrous climate change (not withstanding the already observed dangerous effects mentioned above), or arguments that the risen CO_2 levels will benefit agriculture because plants grow better with more CO_2. These arguments ignore the inherent danger of the gigantic experiment we, as a species, are conducting with our planet: We are changing the composition of the atmosphere, so much so that between 1950 and 2030 the fraction of CO_2 in the atmosphere will have risen by about 33 %.

A third argument is economical and driven by interests that wish to retain the status quo. These interests are, of course, the oil, gas and coal industries, who have disproportionate power in many governments (for example, at the present time, in Canada, the United States, Mexico, all oil-producing middle Eastern countries including Saudi Arabia, the Gulf States, Iran and Iraq, and the tropical countries Nigeria, Venezuela and Indonesia). The political and financial power of these interests is such that they can either control, or at least wield undue influence on elections and governments, and through the media they manipulate the public in their interest. There are TV commercials touting the benefits of "clean coal" and "ethical oil", and there are News Channels (for example, Fox News) that openly propagate the idea that "climate change is a hoax." The essence of the argument is that economical efforts to move from a fossil-fuel driven world economy to one driven by sustainable energy sources would be prohibitively expensive and not necessary in the first place.

Sadly, efforts made by some societies show that it would be quite feasible to make the switch- it is mostly the initial investment that is the problem; once the solar capacities, wind farms and energy storage facilities (hydro-electrical systems, car batteries, synthetic gas storage plants, possibly some nuclear power) are in place, energy could be produced indefinitely for centuries, without the impact on climate and environment we presently face. It is much to our discredit that the present generation is failing to address the problem, and leaves the fallout to you, the class of 2030, and your children.

4.3   No Trespassing

We have seen earlier how our cities and societies are being fractured by the gated community idea. Unfortunately, the phenomenon does not end at the city's edge. Low energy (gasoline) prices have given birth to a culture of ever growing suburbs and exurbs, and a significant percentage of the population spends hours every day in long commutes from and to their homes. Further, the land laws in much of North America are such that development in the sense of construction of private homes and exclusion of the public can happen in places which carry economic or recreational value for society, such as farmlands or mountain forests. Mansions on mountain tops are all too commonplace in parts of California, and usable farmland is being converted into malls or rows of townhouses as I write this. This is a process which is clearly not sustainable (as we are going to run out of land sooner or later).

Land use, in the form in which I intend to criticize it here, consists of two connected steps: First, the management of agricultural or forest lands, be they public or private, and second, the sale and development of bits and pieces of these lands into suburbia. I will treat the two separately, although they are closely linked.

4.3.1   Development.

Let us begin by stating that there is a need for housing, and that people have to live somewhere. Citizens also have the choice to live where they can afford to make a living, and *where their settlement is compatible with the community interest.*

It is the latter which is widely ignored in North America, where private land ownership with all its inherent rights was always held high. This was fine while a huge, empty continent was there to be settled (that is was never empty and that the land was taken or bought, for a pittance, from the First Nations, is a separate story), but it is a policy that is long overdue for revision. Already it is all too obvious what happens without policy changes: places like Southern California, Southwest Florida, or parts of New England have

been developed to such a degree that parkland and farmland are becoming scarce, habitat loss for many species is
critical, and the remaining forests, grasslands or undeveloped coast are under permanent pressure. Actually, it is
even worse than that: much of what has been developed
is in the form of planned (often gated) communities, separated by highways, strip malls and commercial and industrial districts. The automobile is the only possible means
of transportation, and much of the land is sacrificed for its
storage (parking) and motion (in some areas 70%). This
phenomenon exists in or near most North American cities,
and is being replicated around the world.

This has happened in the name of individual freedom
and prosperity: the freedom to buy land wherever you wish,
the freedom to private home ownership on that land and the
freedom to commute in a private vehicle. The irony is that
such freedom of the individual leads to a tragic impediment
of the freedom of all. Symptoms are all around us. Here
are two examples.

In the early 2000s Hollywood released a movie titled
"Cold Mountain" and relating a tragic story happening
during the American civil war (by the way, a movie worth
seeing in this author's unqualified opinion). Much of the
movie is set in the Appalachian mountains (where the tit-
ular town of Cold Mountain is supposedly located), but as
I read about the making of the movie I was flabbergasted
to discover that they had to go to the Carpathian mountains in Romania to find a mountain range similar to the
Appalachians, but *sufficiently undeveloped* to pass for the

Appalachians in the 1860s. Such has uncontrolled development of land in America affected the landscape, that one could no longer find a few valleys in the Appalachians in 2000 which can be made to resemble what it used to look like.

A few years ago we traveled through the State of New Hampshire, where the license plates are adorned with the slogan "Live Free or Die" (really). As we drove along on the crowded highway, following one of these license plates, I could not help but notice that all the land along the highway was gated off, and "Keep out" and "No Trespassing" signs were everywhere. At least along this highway, I formed the strong impression that in their quest to live free at all cost, the citizens of New Hampshire have lost the freedom to go anywhere but their own house, the shopping mall or one of the public parks. In their worship of privacy and private property, afraid of strangers walking on their land, they have restricted the freedom of movement for the general public, and implicitly for themselves. Such is the irony of private safety and rights, that it cuts into the very freedom concept on which America was founded.

More recently, I saw encroachment of similar development in Southwest Florida, where the lands surrounding the Everglades are under assault. Farm lands and habitat of flamingoes, black bear and the rare Florida panther have been turned into gated communities, members' only golf courses and strip malls.

It does not have to be that way. In much of Europe, where land is scarce and of high community value, access to forest lands for recreational (but non-intrusive) purposes is open and free. This means that you can walk, picnic, bird watch, etc., but not hunt, use an ATV, or chop down trees. Nevertheless, they have land laws that control land use much more strictly. If they didn't, Europe would be urban sprawl from Denmark to Sicily and from Bordeaux to Warsaw. Yet they have huge forests, mostly in private hands, with managed (hunted) wildlife and public access for recreation (hiking, cycling, picnics and the like). Over there, owning a piece of land simply does not mean that you can develop or keep the public out. Some cities in the U.S. are beginning to pass laws in the same spirit (Davis, California, was a pioneer), but it is late, much too late.

Where will you go to see the world as it was, Class of 2030?

4.3.2 In my own back yard: the wild coast of Vancouver island.

My home is in Victoria, the capital city of BC, located at the southern tip of Vancouver Island. Much of the island is forest, and much of this forest is considered an industrial forest in the sense of wood production. Large timber companies hold licenses to harvest the trees, and they also largely control the access to these forests. A lot has been written about logging practices which have led to clear-cutting of much of the old-growth forest, and its replacement by tree cultures consisting largely of one or two species of trees, all of the same age.[1] But I digress.

What I really wish to write about in this section, as a case study, is the manipulation of tree farm licensed and private forest lands on southern Vancouver Island. A little background is necessary to understand the issue.

The forest lands in my province are either privately owned or belong to the "Crown" (which is a euphemism for the province, i.e., the people). Crown land is in principle accessible to all, but private land is, of course, not. Matters become confused when such lands are adjacent and belong to or are managed by the same timber company, as is the case on the southern coast here. Historically, a company called Western Forest Products owned the coastal strip and the very beautiful coast line west of Victoria, while the more elevated lands to the north belonged to the province, i.e., were and still are Crown lands. A contract was signed more than half a century ago which provided Western Forest Products a tree farm license to much of these lands; this contract included an obligation of WFP to include the privately owned strip in the licenses in the sense that it had to be treated in the same way as the Crown land; it could be harvested but had to be replanted, and access of the public

---

[1]This monoculture approach has greatly contributed to an environmental and economic catastrophe in the BC interior, namely, the northern pine beetle infestation of the forest on the central BC plateau. On an area the size of England the forest has been killed by these insects. There are arguments regarding the origin of the problem, but the simplest and most convincing reasons are that climate change as discussed in a previous section enables the beetles to survive the warmer winters, and the forest is affected so badly because it contains exactly the species and age distribution of trees the pine beetles consume. It's a man-made problem from two different points of view.

to these lands had to be guaranteed. And this was the state of affairs until 2008.

In the interim three crucial developments had occurred. First, business was not going very well for WFP. The supply of large trees from the coast, once seemingly inexhaustible, had started to dry up because of over-cutting, and the smaller second or third growth trees were far less lucrative to market. Second, there was now much resistance from the public towards the clear-cutting which had dominated the BC forests until the 1980s. And last, the housing crash and subsequent economic downturn had much reduced the demand for BC lumber and other forest products. So revenue was down.

But then the company owned the coastal strip of land (how they had come to own this is a story by itself, not to be told here for brevity). A remote edge of the BC wilderness in 1960, the wild coast had by now become a jewel in the beautiful outskirts of Victoria. Undeveloped and wild, but only about 1 hour's drive from the capital, and waterfront!

WFP asked the government (the BC Liberal government, a very conservative and business-friendly outfit) whether they could do something about the old rules regarding this land, and Rich Coleman, the responsible minister, allowed them to delete the land from the tree farm licenses and sell it for development. The public was not consulted, and no compensation was asked for or paid. It was as if the government, in deficit as it was, gave a 50 million dollar gift to WFP, because this was a price at which the land was put up for sale.

The BC public rose up in fury, and many environmental organizations began a long and bitter fight to prevent re-zoning of the land for the developer's plans. Remarkably, after a process that lasted several years, the public has prevailed, although as I write this the land is still owned by a developer, and is not safe from clear-cutting or spotty development. The issue is still at a cross-roads.

What if the protests had not happened? What if the land had been freed up for development as desired by the involved private interests, and this development had been tolerated by a complicit government?

Let's come back to BC in 2030. Let us assume that the governing Liberal Party has been elected and reelected and their spirit of "BC is open for business" has prevailed over all those years. The former WFP lands to the west of the city have been sold and developed.

The suburbs of Victoria sprawl from Sidney and Duncan to Port Renfrew. As you drive along the highway past Sooke, you notice that much of the privatized coast is inaccessible and closed to the public. There are gated communities on the coast and in the hills, and the only way to enter is to buy your way in. You have to make reservations months in advance to have a picnic at French Beach, and time slots are given out. Side roads, also gated, climb up the San Juan Ridge, and only residents of designated communities or the logging companies have access to the remaining forests. So if you are an average member of the class of 2030, you are out of luck and can only access a fraction of this coast, a coast which was freely accessible to my generation, a generation that let this happen.

But wait... I am writing hypothetically. At least for this example, it looks as if the coast will be spared. Enough people have engaged in opposition towards the development plans to make a difference. It is an example which shows what is possible. It raises hope for the future.

4.4 Globalization

A few years ago we needed to buy new baseboards for a home renovation. A visit to the local hardware and carpentry store (called Windsor Plywood; it still exists, though no longer bears that name) offered white baseboards of good quality, at 35 cents a foot. We were attended to by older, experienced salesmen, who offered competent advice but seemed somewhat subdued— The Home Depot had recently opened a franchise just out of town, less than a 10 km drive away. Already the smaller stores were "feeling the heat": Home Depot offered similar baseboards (which we ended up buying, though the quality turned out to be poorer) at 32 cents a foot.

If this story sounds familiar, it should. A global market place and inexpensive transportation methods (albeit with a large carbon footprint and increased demands on roads) have generated many gigantic chains of superstores, which flood the consumer with goods produced in China, India or Mexico (or, more generally, where labour is cheap). We flock to these stores for the cheap TV sets, the low prices on meat or vegetables, or the lower gas prices. In my city of Victoria we have Walmart, Costco, the Great Canadian Superstore, and two Home Depot stores.

I shop there myself. It is indeed true that the selection is astounding, and the prices are low. It is usually difficult to find someone to give advice, and shopping expeditions take a long time because of the driving, parking and shopping itself. Invariably, there are long walks along long aisles, followed by long lineups at the checkout stations, followed by loading expeditions and the drive back home. Using public transit is possible in some cases but impractical for many reasons.

The implications for our society, however, are dire. First, the megastores drive smaller retailers out of business. This implies contraction of small business and loss of jobs, as we indeed observed with Windsor Plywood. Second, most production lines are now outsourced to the third world: manufactured goods are much cheaper to produce in China, India, or Bangladesh, where, for example, Indian factory workers move from the impoverished countryside in Orissa or Rajasthan to the factories on the outskirts of Delhi, Jaipur or Mumbai. I saw the multitudes of such workers during a visit to Delhi, walking, cycling or riding overcrowded buses to their employer. An inquiry from my part informed me that the typical pay for a month is about $ 150.00, a salary which is insufficient for a half-decent living even in India. A factory worker cannot afford much of anything for such wages; they share housing or sleep on the street, and own next to nothing. From many a fraction of the money is sent home to destitute families, who stayed on land that can no longer feed its tenants.

The western worker cannot possibly compete with this production model. Products produced in such a system will of necessity be much cheaper than what can be produced at home, and can be imported at low or negligible cost into Canada, the US or Western Europe. Services which can be provided over the internet can likewise be exported—services which used to be located in Los Angeles or Toronto are now offered from Bangalore or Mumbai.

Globalization has thus provided employment where none previously existed. It has also led to increased exploitation of the poor and destruction of middle and lower class jobs in the western world. The goods and services thus created are being sold to all of us.

There are many hidden costs for society, and in particular for the tax payer. First, there is un– or underemployment in places which used to offer good middle class jobs, with benefits, 20 years ago. Workers in, say, the automobile parts industry used to make 30 dollars an hour, with benefits. The company could not compete with its third–world competition and had to shut down, laying everybody off. Now, a new company has taken over the old location, making a new product, and they can and do hire for 9 dollars an hour, with no benefits. There are plenty of takers.

Then there are the added energy and space costs of off-shore manufacturing and distribution in megastores: transportation and distribution costs, access roads to the suburban megastores, land use for their parking lots. Manufacture and distribution on a local and smaller scale would reduce all of the above, but... it would drive up the cost of products because the locally employed people would command a higher wage than the underpaid third world factory worker.

If you, member of the class of 2030, have read to here, you have probably already figured out that you stand a good chance of being unemployed exactly because your job is being done offshore, for a wage that you could not survive from in your home town.

4.5   Targets to Miss

Let us assume for a moment that the troubling trends discussed in the previous chapters continue without any counteraction. Where would that leave us in 2030? Are there societies on the planet that have gone further down the path of no community spirit and no generational contracts?

It is not hard to find examples; depending on their geographical location and history, they differ in their present state, but all of them can be described to some extent by the term "failed state". Extreme cases of failed states are Somalia and Pakistan, where religious fundamentalism (in this case, the Muslim type) and chronically corrupt governments have resulted in a general collapse of society structure. The results are well known: these countries cannot appropriately feed their people, education and medical systems are inadequate to say the least, banditry and terrorism thrive. Other examples of societies at or beyond the brink of "failed state" include many other African countries.

In this year of 2012 the countries of southern Europe, especially Greece, are suffering a severe financial and economic crisis. It is a European crisis because of the common currency, the EURO, which was adopted by Greece a decade ago and provided the country and its society access to huge amounts of liquidity. However, as widespread tax evasion appears to be a way of life in Greece (and, for that matter, in Italy), the loans Greece received from the rest of Europe are unlikely to be ever paid back.

This is a variation of the subprime crisis we visited in Chapter 1; the problem is that the system faces collapse once the credit flow stops, which has now happened. The austerity measures which Greece has had to put in effect are exceedingly harsh on it citizens, be they unemployed youths, seniors, small business owners, or school teachers. The country which invented democracy and mathematics is on the brink of falling back to third-world status; its wealthy elite, 1,000 (or so) families, keep their wealth hidden in Swiss or Cayman island bank accounts, while the middle class and the poor suffer the consequences of a collective delusion.

Our narrative mentioned many other symptoms of failure present in the west but abounding in various societies around the globe: the abundance of gated communities in Mexico; the failure of tax collection in societies from Greece to Argentina to Russia; the disregard for the environment in places like Nigeria.

There are societies which deal better with these problems. South Korea invests heavily in education and social programs, and their infrastructure is highly developed. Germany's economic success depends largely on a very versatile and inclusive education system, and an industrial sector which draws skilled labour from this system. The Scandinavian countries tax their citizens heavily but reinvest the revenue into solid and universal social and educational services.

Chapter 5

Freedom, Restraint and Hypocrisy

The title terms in this final chapter of my narrative play a big part in the stories I have told. I have pointed out repeatedly how aspirations to be free can actually lead to restrictions of freedom. There are obvious dangers to society, and implicitly to all its members, if you empower citizens to avoid taxes, to occupy large tracts of land for personal purposes, or to pollute common space, water or air. The meaning of freedom must of necessity be constrained by laws in order to permit a truly empowered society, be it laws that regulate the bearing of firearms, the use of motor vehicles on agricultural lands, or the disposal of waste products. We have never had the right to dump our waste in our neighbour's garden, and most of us would not even contemplate doing so. It is in this sense that a civil free society must also be a responsible society.

A related and important concept are contracts. Societies which plan for more than the day realize that long-term investments in education, health and social security are necessary not only to guarantee individual happiness and prosperity, but also societal stability. Breaking the underlying contracts may save a lot of money short-term, but leads to structural problems (as seen in "failed states") over generational time scales. Stable societies will implement systems which guarantee that future generations can obtain the training they need to propagate their functionality; in turn, the older generation will be able to count on functional medical and pension services. And in the future, we will need systems which amount to "contracts with the planet" to propagate the viability of our environment for our livelihood. Such systems will have to control the amounts of emissions, the use of land and water, and the type of transportation we use.

Restraint is a necessary ingredient in such a utopian successful society. There were times in the 1960s when economic and industrial progress appeared so rapid that unlimited prosperity and mobility for all were considered a reality for the near future; how easy it was to predict that nuclear power would become so commonplace that energy supplies would be all but free. We watched the moon landings and mused about scientific discoveries which would make interstellar travel possible within our lifetimes. The emerging environmental problems (at that time mostly water and air pollution) were largely dismissed as temporary glitches, soon to be resolved with technological progress.

As we know from hindsight, matters did not pan out that way. Nuclear power has not kept its promise, the stars are as far away as ever, and the planet is under severe man-made stress. And yet, much of our behaviour in the west has not adapted to the realities. We talk about the need to cut back, but only cost will drive us to reduce our impact on the environment. The contradiction between what many of us say and how we actually behave regarding to environmental conduct can only be described as hypocrisy.

You may now feel reprimanded, but I should freely admit that I am a hypocrite in this sense myself. I have discussed the perils of climate change and the dangers of fossil fuel use and transport. Yet, I use fossil fuels a lot; my personal worst offence is air travel, the wonderful way in which I can be in Victoria today and in Seoul tomorrow. Much of my travel is for professional reasons, but some is for pleasure. Two intercontinental flights a year contribute (as my share) several tons of CO_2 to the greenhouse burden uploaded to the atmosphere. My driving, by comparison, is modest—I commute by bicycle or bus, and fill up my gas tank only once in six weeks or so. But mobility, be it by individual gas-fuelled vehicle or by jet, has become a major defining feature of most of us. We even offend in our efforts to deal with the very problem: Major conferences on climate change (the most recent one in Copenhagen) are attended by many thousands of delegates, most traveling by jet plane with the corresponding massive CO_2 emissions.

Is this necessary? More and more, I think not. There are industries (travel agencies, air lines, hotel chains) which profit from our hypocritical behaviour, and as the behaviour entails a lot of fun and entertainment, we are reluctant to cut back. Who wants to take the bus to a nearby ranch for a vacation, when in a few short hours you can fly to an exotic distant location promising exciting food and adventure?

It would be nice to be able to cut out the air travel; there does not seem to be an easy alternative, though; we live in a huge country with limited train and bus service. There also seems to be little hope to arrive at vastly improved fuel efficiency [10], not unless dirigibles will make a comeback. It is a problem which offers, at this time, no easy solution. The simplest short-term steps may be to tax aviation fuel and force people to fly less by that measure.

All of us should apply restraint in our use of energy, and in our use of space and resources. There are crucial lifestyle choices to be made regarding the use and sharing of resources, and restraint will inevitably be a necessity in these choices.

Individual restraint is desirable but likely not good enough. We will need government action such as taxation of certain behaviours (carbon taxes, etc.), and we will need massive investments in new sustainable technologies.

Chapter 6

Epilogue

And so we have reached the end of the litany, or so it must seem to you. I am trying to visualize what you, young reader of the class of 2030, will think and feel should you read this in, say, 2029, as you approach graduation. Has my pessimistic view to the future transformed into reality?

Frankly, the writing of this letter, triggered as it was by a feeling of depression and powerlessness, has only deepened these feelings in me. You, of course, have the advantage of hindsight, and maybe you can read and dismiss my vision as the bad dream of a previous generation.

There are signs of hope around me. The problems alluded to in the chapters of this book are front and centre in the news these days. The great droughts in the US and India in the summer of 2012, which augur food shortages for the months and years to come, have all but silenced the deniers of climate change. Real science may still get its day, and politics will have to address the CO_2 issue out of necessity. Climate change has also resurfaced in the American media as an underlying reason why hurricane 'Sandy', which devastated the mid-Atlantic coast of the U.S. in the fall of 2012, could grow to the size it reached and cause the estimated $ 50 billion in damages it left behind. As I write this, President Barack Obama has just been re-elected for a second term, and it is to be hoped that his administration will make a genuine effort to address this problem.

There is a realization in a large fraction of the public that the tax cutting philosophy of neoconservatives has failed and only benefitted the upper classes. There are even members of these classes who call for higher taxes for the benefit of society. There are louder and stronger calls for financial regulation as created in the 1930s, and there is pressure by society for more stable and universal health and social systems.

I see much promise in the young, who rise against the old ways in anger and frustration. There are many others who care and engage in social or environmental activism by joining political parties, citizens' initiatives against controversial developments, or environmental movements. The discourse among academics is alive and well, and they need to assert their insights with political leaders.

There are signs of change in our society. Letters in newspapers depict awareness and concern about the changing climate and its dire implications. A culture of recycling has sprung up and reduced the flow of materials into landfills. The "Great North Pacific Plastic Garbage Vortex" is realized as a symptom of our waning wasteful ways. Green corridors are being created in and around many cities, and more parks and more wildlife provide respite from our artificial environments. People make more environmental choices in their shopping and eating habits, like the 100-mile diet. Other lifestyle choices pointing into the right direction include more cycling and walking for daily commutes, reduced air travel, and volunteering for beach cleanups and the like.

So it may well be that what I wrote about is turning around, and that the world in which you graduate will be a world in which your options and freedoms are many. You may have gone through a complete and well-balanced public school education. It may be that you live in a city or neighbourhood which is in itself or is part of a community, where citizens care about each other and about their environment. It may be that you have "green" choices for your transportation, your housing and your eating habits, and that you have learned and appreciate how to live in harmony with the nature around you.

Acknowledgement. I could not be where and what I am without my parents. My mother taught me the value of education and the importance of a clear and honest world view. My father taught me to be truthful, and by sharing his love for the natural world gave me the drive to preserve and improve.

In my wife Leslie I found a partner who shares all these values. She is the steady anchor of my life, moving things along while I can dream.

I have had and still have the fortune to have many friends and colleagues who inspire me with their insight, their critical minds, kindness, and support. Special Thanks to the lunch group from the University and to my friends from the Alpine Club of Canada. Our many conversations were seeds for this book.

I am grateful to Teresita Hernandes-Quesada for the cover design and her assistance with the design. Thanks also to Reinel Sospedra Alfonso.

Bibliography

[1] Barth, James R., Li, Tong, and Lu, Wenling: Bank Regulation in the United States. CESifo Economic Studies, 2009, di:10.1093/cesifo/ifp026

[2] Dobbs, Lou: War on the Middle Class. Viking (2006)

[3] The Globe and Mail, May 10, 2012: Harper is right: Foreign Radicals are after the oil sands

[4] Lewis, Michael: The Big Short. W.W. Norton (2010)

[5] Lewis, Michael: Boomerang. W.W. Norton (2011)

[6] http://www.opensecrets.org/lobby/top.php?indexType=c

[7] http://www.opposingviews.com/i/religion/christianity/catholicism/rick santorum says he clings bibles and guns

[8] en.wikipedia.org/wiki/Ronald_Reagan

[9] The Wikipedia page on Prop 13

[10] Mackay, David: Sustainable Energy – Without the Hot Air, http://www.withouthotair.com/

[11] The Globe and Mail, July 10, 2012

[12] http://www.economist.com/node/21558303

www.ingramcontent.com/pod-product-compliance
Lightning Source LLC
Chambersburg PA
CBHW072249310526
45795CB00011B/580